Haiku Circus

BASED ON THE TRADITIONAL FORM OF JAPANESE POETRY

Haiku Circus

ISBN-13 978-1466321465
ISBN-10 1466321466

Printed in the United States of America

Haiku Circus has appeared in the following publications:

- University of Alaska Anchorage The Northern Light
- University of Alaska Fairbanks's The Sun Star
- Slippery Rock University's The Rocket
- University of South Carolina's The Daily Gamecock
- The College of St. Scholastica's The Cable
- Cornell University's Daily Sun
- Simon Fraser University's The Peak
- Glendale Community College's The Voice
- University of Massachusetts Boston's The Mass Media
- Drake University's The Times Delphic
- Ngee Ann Polytechnic's The Urban Wire (Indonesia)
- Indiana University's Northwest Phoenix
- Fort Lewis College's The Independent
- Worcester Polytechnic Institute's Tech News
- Wayne State University's The South End
- Lakeland College's the Lakeland Mirror
- The University of North Carolina at Asheville's The Blue Banner
- Bemidji State University's Northern Student
- Lock Haven University's The Eagle Eye

Original newspapers in 2003:

- UNLV's Rebel Yell
- University of Scranton's The Aquinas
- Centennial College's The Courier
- International University Bremen's IUB Crossroads
- Muhlenberg College's the Muhlenberg Advocate
- American University's The Eagle
- Arizona State University's Web Devil
- Ohio Wesleyan University's The Transcript
- Pima Community College's Aztec Press
- Southern Illinois University Carbondale's Daily Egyptian
- Florida Community College at Jacksonville's The Campus Voice

also:

The L Magazine
Live Ink (textbook)
fbx square (Fairbanks)
The C-Ville Weekly

TABLE OF CONTENTS

1.
SUCH IS LIFE

FLA. CRUISE '99

It was a fun trip
but for now that film stays lost
in your junk drawer.

"Hey, Ma! Where's the broom?!"

Dream big, but know this:
Despite all of your wishing
some dreams don't come true.

FLA. CRUISE '99
It was a fun trip...
5
...but for now that film stays lost...
7
...in your junk drawer.
5

"Hey, Ma! Where's the broom?!"
Dream big, but know this:
5
despite all of your wishing...
7
some dreams don't come true.
5

The Rapture is Not Upon Us

Some can't accept that
the world will continue on
after they are gone.

When Civil Discussions Go Bad

"It's not that simple."
"This war is Israel's fault!"
"Grape Juice, how could you?"

The Rapture is Not Upon Us

When Civil Discussions Go Bad

"What happened to your face!?!"

Once when I was young
I saw my parents "do it".
I puked my eyes out.

Self-Diagnosis

What's this over here?
I've never seen it before.
Could it be cancer?

"What happened to your face!?!"

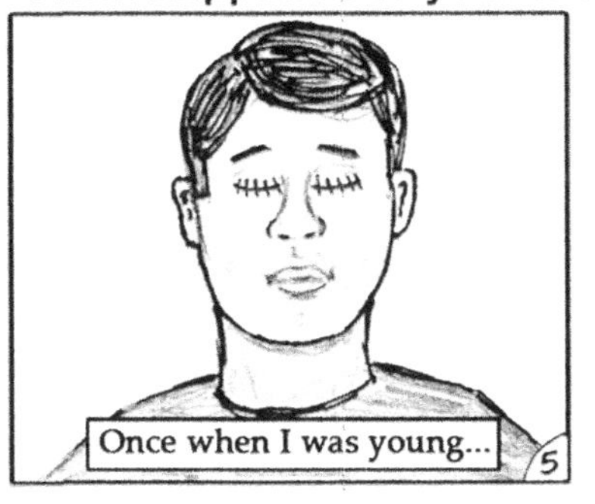

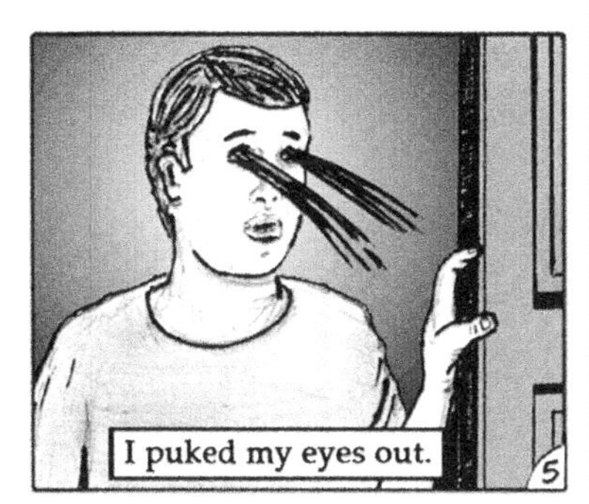

Self-Diagnosis

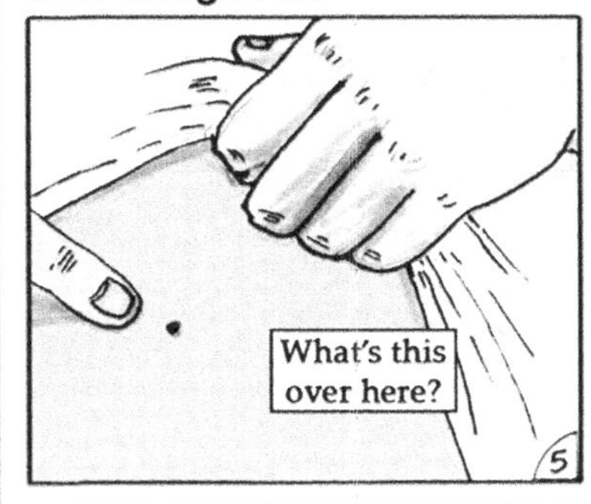

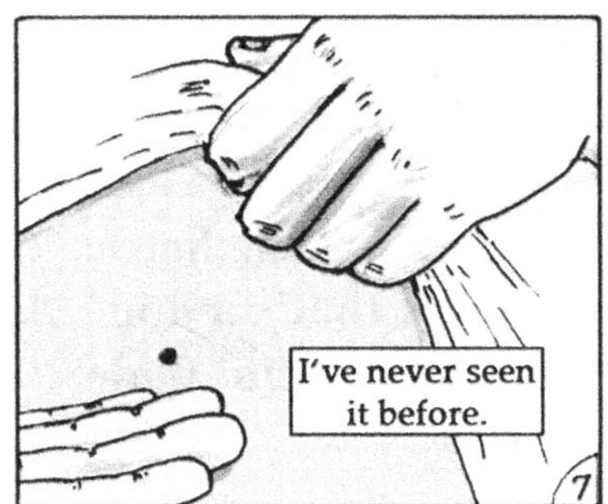

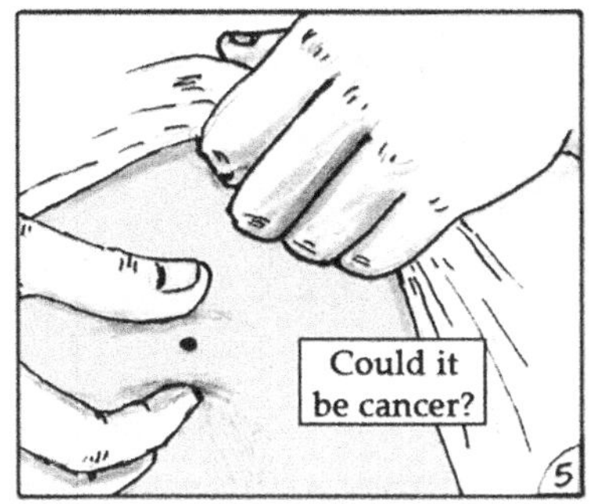

A Sunny Sunday Afternoon

I bought myself grapes
some dollar store sunglasses
and had a picnic.

Gender Ambiguity in Stick People

"Check out the hottie."
"Um... I think that's a dude, dude."
"Who you callin' dude?!"

A Sunny Sunday Afternoon

Gender Ambiguity in Stick People

The Boy Who was Swinging and Kept on Going

No one's here to watch.
And look how high I can go!
They'll all be sorry.

The Answers of the Universe

A fortune cookie.
What wisdom might it bestow?
"You are holding this."

The Boy Who was Swinging and Kept on Going

The Answers of the Universe

Sing Your Life

These are all my shoes.
My one spoon and my one fork.
I'm a bachelor.

A Different Perspective

Beautiful? Ugly?
Everyone looks the same when
seen from outer space.

Sing Your Life

A Different Perspective

Afraid of Boys

Go on... talk to him.
You'll regret it if you don't.
You can do better.

Family Dynamics in the Year 2031

"I got two mothers."
"Cool. I have orgy-parents.
Four moms and three dads."

Afraid of Boys

Family Dynamics in the Year 2031

We Go Way Back

Somewhere while you sleep,
your imaginary friend
wishes you would call.

Same Difference

No one danced with me.
Not even Acne-Arnold.
I'm so ugly... jinx!

We Go Way Back

Same Difference

"Mom? Dad? Please don't put my pet raccoon, Crackers, to sleep."

**In closing, I ask
wouldn't I keep you alive
if you had rabies?**

"You say tomato, I say..."

**"No son of mine is--"
"I can't change who I am, Dad.
I'm fruit, dammit. Fruit!"**

"Mom? Dad? Please don't put my pet raccoon, Crackers, to sleep."

"You say tomato, I say..."

"They're gonna tear down the factory and build an orphanage!"

"But what can we do?"
"I know... Let's have a bake sale!"
"Pollution is saved!"

Conversation

"What?" "Nothing." "Sorry?"
"You were saying?" "After you."
"I insist." "Yeah." "Huh?"

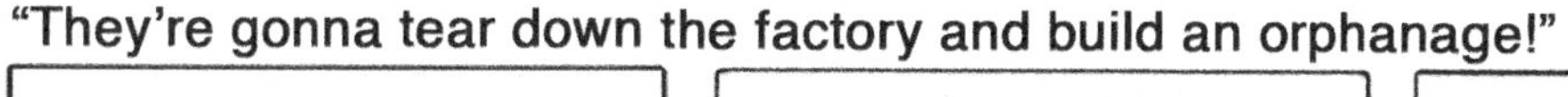

Conversation

"Oh, the baby!"

"He's crawling now too.
Isn't he adorable?"
"He wants his mother."

2.
SCIENCE FICTION
(a.k.a. Robots, Aliens, Space & Monsters)

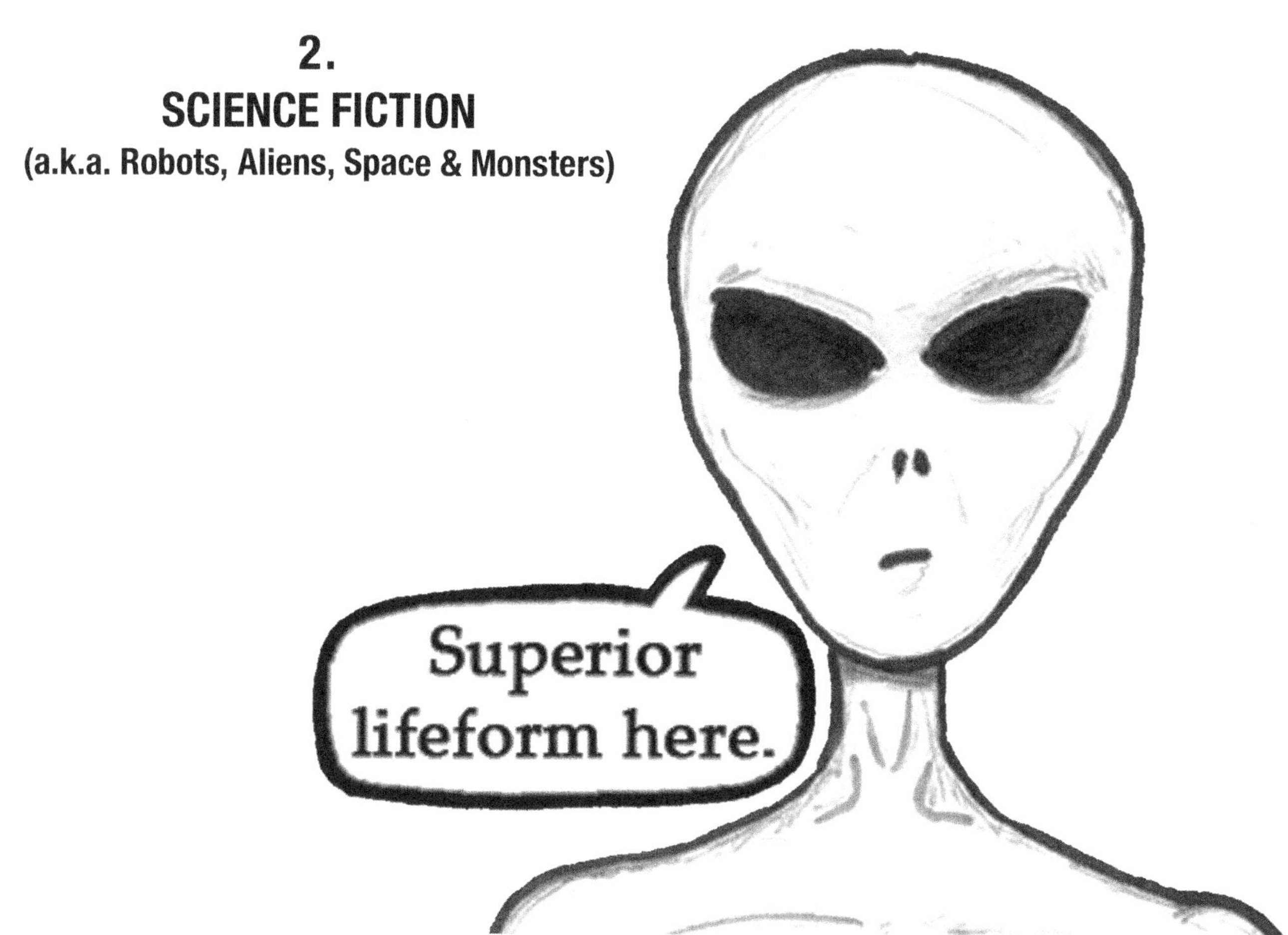

Cliffhangers... in Space!
(to be continued)

"A black hole." "Oh no!"
"Oh no!" "It's sucking us in."
"A space shark." "Oh no!"

That New Girl

"May I have this dance?"
"You may. Can I abduct you?"
"Sure!" "Margot is pleased."

Cliffhangers... in Space! (to be continued)

That New Girl

"Look out! Gamma Rays!"

"Halt or I'll shoot you.
With my top secret GAY-RUN."
"Well, I'm off. Toodles!"

Don't Litter

Trash-Bot is lonely.
Will Trash-Bot ever find love?
Trash-Bot says, "Thank you."

"Look out! Gamma Rays!"

Don't Litter

Vroomba: The Vacuum Robot

"I sure love my wife."
"But I'll tell her tomorrow."
Meanwhile... outer space

Robot Wars

Doctor Tom's robots
hurt humans instead of helped.
'Cuz he's dyslexic.

Vroomba: The Vacuum Robot

Robot Wars

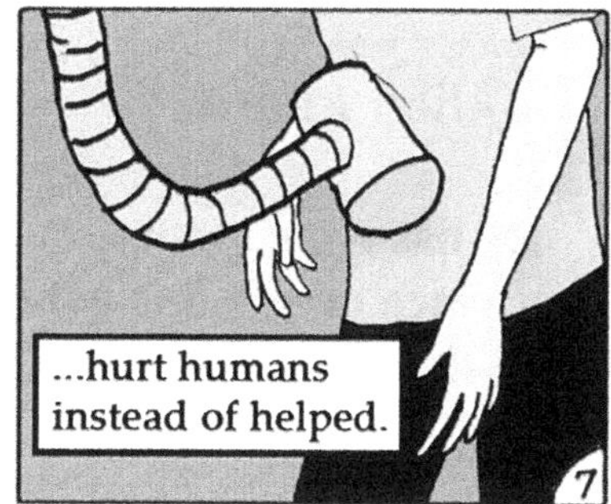

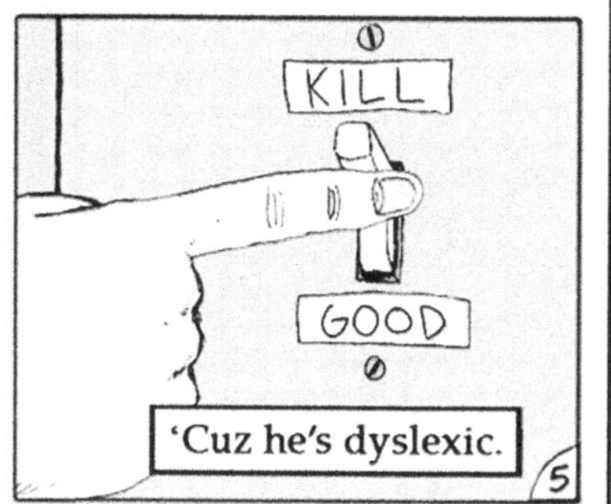

IT CAME FROM THE WOMB!

So many babies.
But which one's the alien?
ALEIN BABY!

Alien Adultery

He has been gloomy
ever since he saw his wife
in that motel room.

IT CAME FROM THE WOMB!

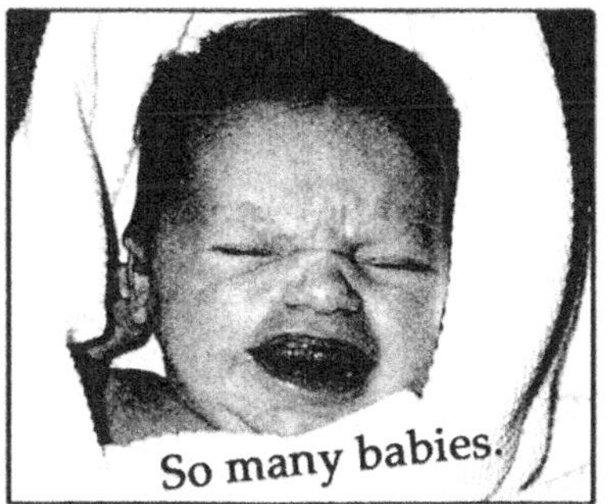

Alien Adultery

The Earth Stood Still

**Well, hello Earthlings.
Superior lifeform here.
Take me to your Bush*.**

A Brief History of the Universe

**First, there was nothing.
Then there were a lot of things.
Then... nothing again.**

*the 43rd U.S. president

The Earth Stood Still

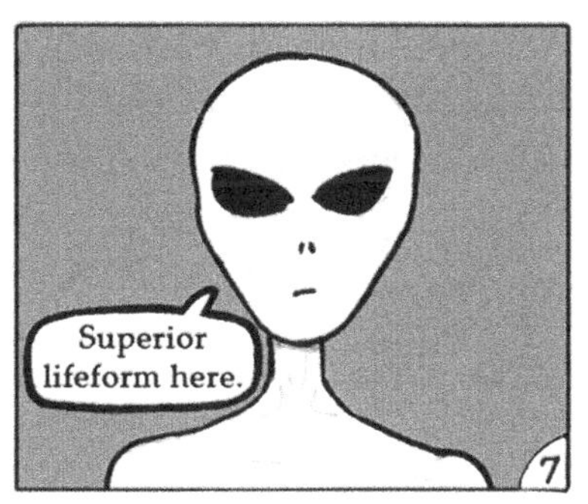

A Brief History of the Universe

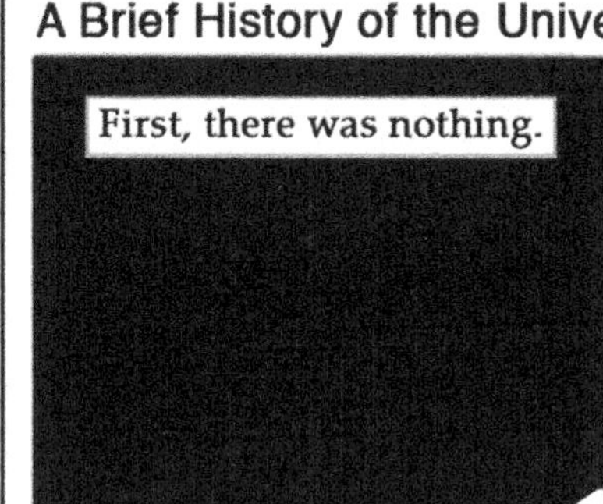

Resolutions... in Space!

"We're goners." "But wait.
My time machine." "But where to?"
"To Kokomo." "Rad."

A Child's Nightmare

You're getting sleepy...
feel relaxed. Nice and relaxed."
"Sleep tight, little one."

Resolutions... in Space!

A Child's Nightmare

Natural Selection

The Alpha Donut
didn't stand a chance against
the Alpha Rodent.

4th Grade Horror Stories

This fifth grade teacher...
Her head fell off during class.
And... she... kept teaching.

Natural Selection

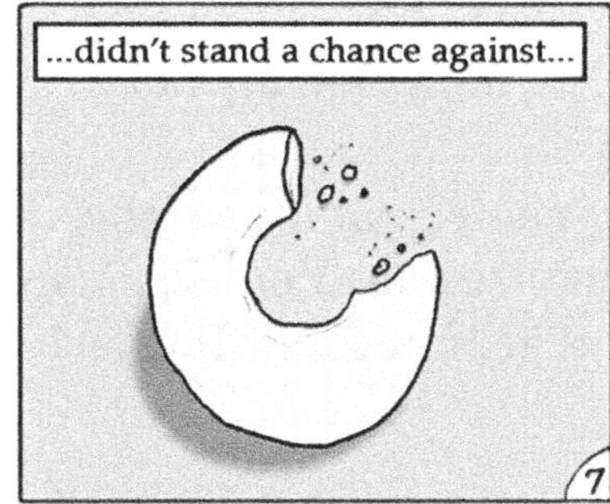

4th Grade Horror Stories

Monster Squad

You're not my mother.
I recognize you. You're... You're...
The Squiggle-Monster!

Omniscient Being

"Earthlings, I know all.
I know all of you will die!"
"You tricked us with words."

Monster Squad

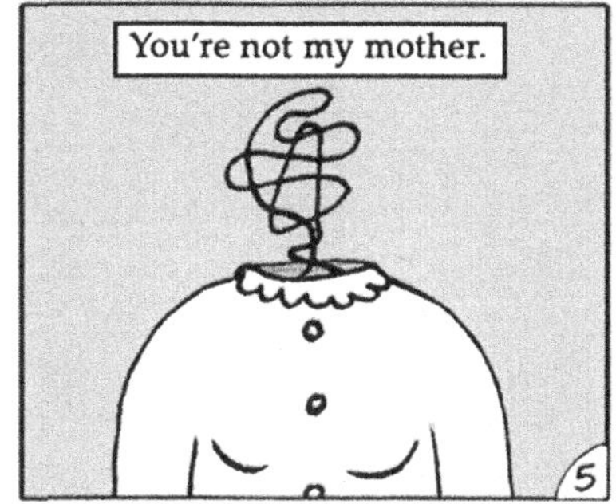

Omniscient Being

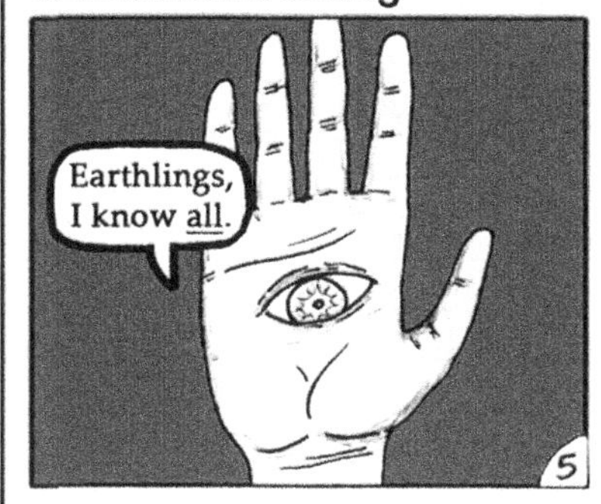

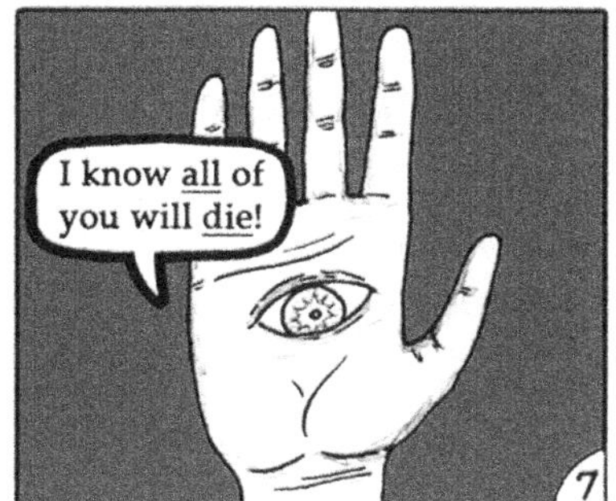

"Can't sleep..."

I dream of monsters.
And the worst part of it is
they're made of candy

The Further Adventures of Zpencer Jackson

"Wonder where this goes..."
Zpencer plummets down the hole.
"This place is crazy!"

"Can't sleep..."

The Further Adventures of Zpencer Jackson

MAYDAY, MAYDAY

Good day, passengers.
We're about to encounter
some slight turbulence.

NOVUS ORDO SECULORUM

I can see Heather.
There's Tom, Beth... I see Robert.
I see everyone.

MAYDAY, MAYDAY
Good day, passengers.
5
We're about to encounter...
7
...some slight turbulence.
5

NOVUS ORDO SECLORUM
I can see Heather.
5
There's Tom, Beth... I see Robert.
7
I see everyone.
5

Horror Drawings

"I am Evil-Pen.
I draw only evil things."
"Grrrrr... Now I eat you!"

Paranoia

"BOO! Trick or treat." "Waaaaa!"
"Gotcha." "Don't scare mom like that.
I thought you weren't dead."

Horror Drawings

Paranoia

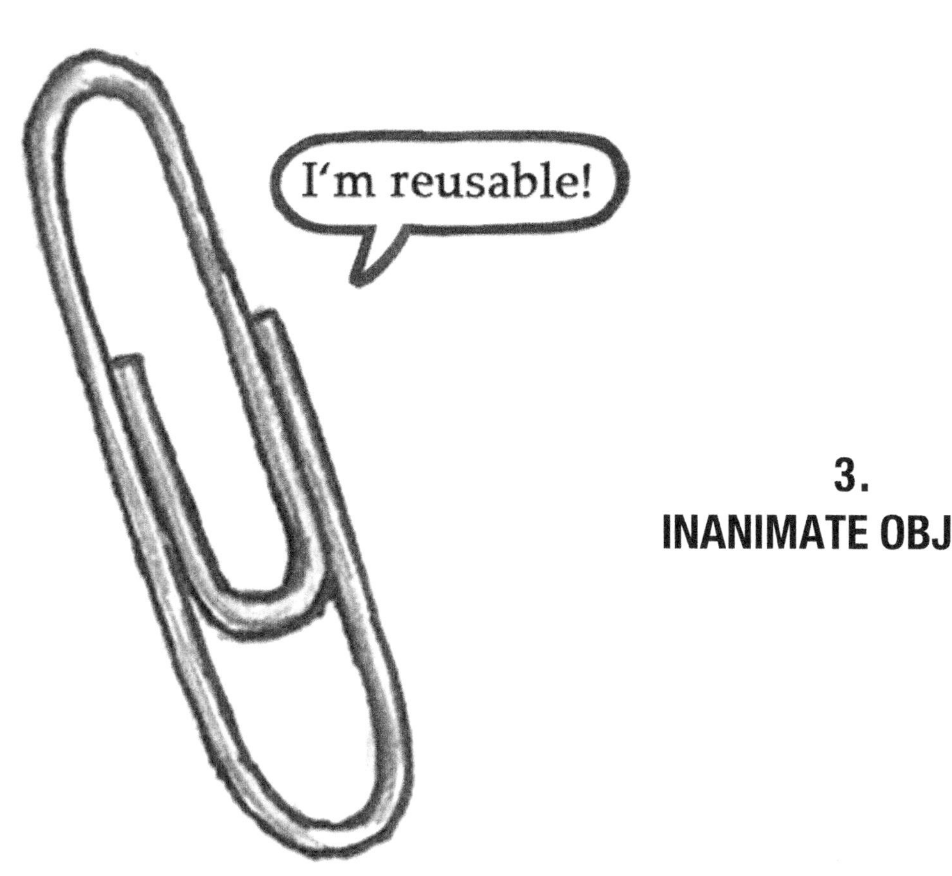

3. INANIMATE OBJECTS

A Kid from the Midwest Moves to the Big City

"What did you call us?"
"Pop." "We're not Pop. We're Sodas.
You hear me, new kid?"

Dirty Socks

"Want to... spice things up?"
"Well what did you have in mind?"
"Hi." "Ooooh." "Yeah?" "Sure." "Nice."

A Kid from the Midwest Moves to the Big City

What did you call us?

5

Pop.

We're not *Pop.* We're Sodas.

7

You hear me, new kid?

5

Dirty Socks

Groooooooooooosss

"I love you, Toothbrush."
"And I love you, Dust-Hairball."
"I'm preggers." "Ba-wha?!?"

A Confederacy of Random Objects

"Proposition 9
all in favor?" "Aye."
"Spool of thread objects."

Grooooooooooosss

A Confederacy of Random Objects

Office Supply Debate Squad

"I'm reusable."
"True. But I think I provide--"
"I'm reusable!"

Office Supply Debate: IRAN

"Diplomacy works.
But we need strict sanctions that..."
"Plan nuclear strikes!"

Office Supply Debate Squad
I'm reusable.
5
True. But I think I provide--
7
I'm reusable!
5

Office Supply Debate: IRAN
Diplomacy works.
5
But we need strict sanctions that...
7
Plan nuclear strikes!
5

Tic-Tac-Toe

Let's see what you got.
Please. That's the best you can do?
Yes! Wait... No? Dammit!!

Tool Feuds

"You're dumb as a nail."
"You hoe." "Takes one to know one."
"Screw you. Screw yourself!"

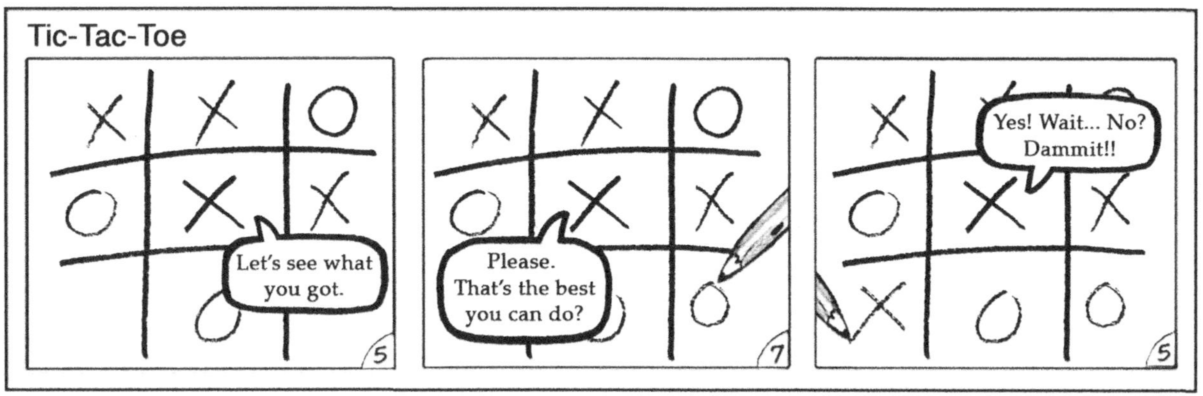
Tic-Tac-Toe
Let's see what you got.
5
Please. That's the best you can do?
7
Yes! Wait... No? Dammit!!
5

Tool Feuds
You're dumb as a nail.
5
You hoe.
Takes one to know one.
7
Screw you.
Screw yourself!
5

Domestic Abuse

"Hey, door. You make a
better door than a window."
"Up yours." "Heh, heh, heh."

Don't Try This at Home

"Hey! This fits in here."
A fancy cat hat for dogs.
Scissor Toothbrushing.

Domestic Abuse

Don't Try This at Home

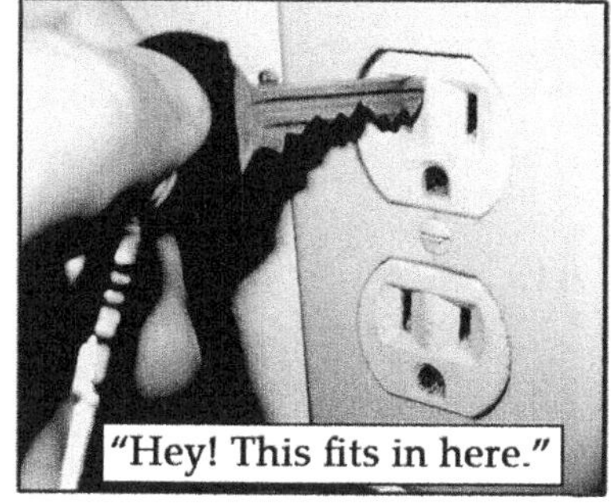

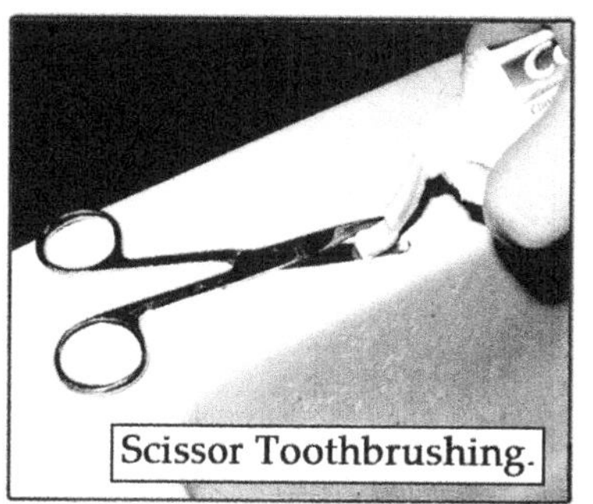

Jello Wars

"I'm calling you out!"
"Years of conflict... it ends here."
"Arrgh! Both of us died!"

"Mr. Bread says..."

When crossing the street
hold hands with an adult... ARRGH!
See you next time, kids.

Jello Wars
I'm calling you out!
5
Years of conflict... it ends here.
7
Arrgh! Both of us died!
5

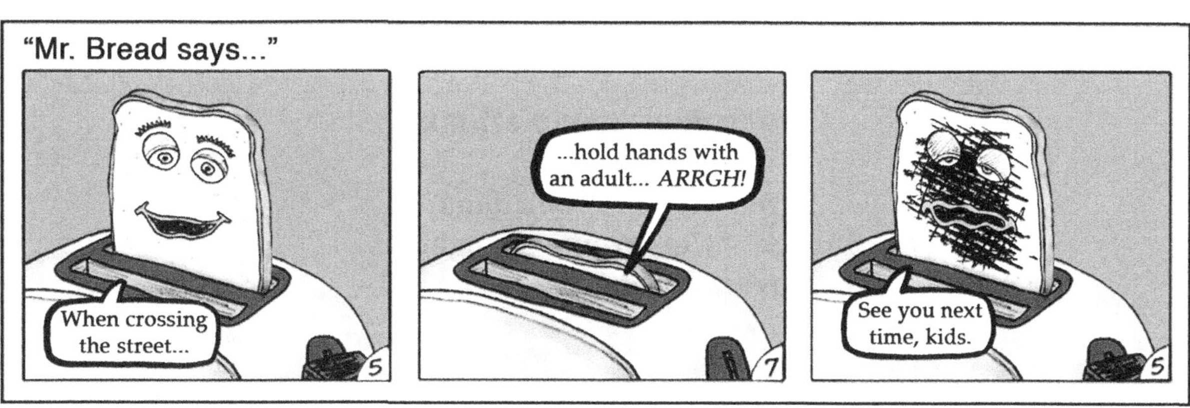
"Mr. Bread says..."
When crossing the street...
5
...hold hands with an adult... ARRGH!
7
See you next time, kids.
5

Modern Love

"It just wouldn't work."
"But, why? Donut, I love you."
"We're not a good fit."

"Keep your hands off me."

"Did you hear something?"
"Huh?" "I'm turning the light on."
"Great. Thanks. Now I'm up!"

Modern Love

"Keep your hands off me."

Beer Pressure

Just one... and that's it.
Come on. One more won't kill ya.
Drive. You can make it.

The Birds and the Bees

"Father?" "Yes, Junior."
"Where do coins come from?" "Ask Mom."
"Mom? "You're adopted."

Beer Pressure

The Birds and the Bees

Innuendo

"How many lightbulbs
does it take to screw in... YOU?"
"Uhh, I guess... one?" "Yes!"

Perspective

"Are we there yet?" "No."
"We've been walking forever."
"Quit all your whining."

Innuendo

Perspective

Get a Room

"Oh button, button
who's got the button? "You do."
"You do." "No, you do."

She's a Maniac!

"What are you doing?
I've never seen you life this."
"Take it like a man."

Get a Room
Oh button, button...
5
...who's got the button?
You do.
7
You do.
No, you do.
5

She's a Maniac!
What are you doing?
5
I've never seen you like this.
7
Take it like a man.
5

Untitled

"We had some good times.
I guess it's best to move on."
But fate wins this round!

4.
POP CULTURE

"Please, don't eat me."

"Oh, no. Not Lunchbox.
No one comes back from Lunchbox."
"No one but Thermos."

Bonus Level

"Sir?" "Leave me alone."
"Just one minute of your time.
Accept Jesus." "No."

"Please, don't eat me."
Oh, no.
Not Lunchbox.
5
No one
comes back
from Lunchbox.
7
No one but Thermos.
5

Bonus Level
Sir?
Leave me
alone.
5
Just one
minute of
your time.
7
Accept
Jesus.
No.
5

"Who's the greatest director of all time?"

"Godard!" "Fellini!"
"Godard!" Fellini!" "Godard!"
"Stephen Spielberg!"

The Hunter and the Hunted

"Look into my eyes.
Feel your eyelids get heavy."
"Wh-wha-what happened?!?"

"Who is the greatest director of all time?"

The Hunter and the Hunted

The Family Blank

**“Pasghetti meatballs
look like poop and poop looks like
pasghetti meatballs.”**

An Alternate Dimension

**My mortality
and thoughts of eternity
keep me up at night.**

The Family *Blank*

An Alternate Dimension

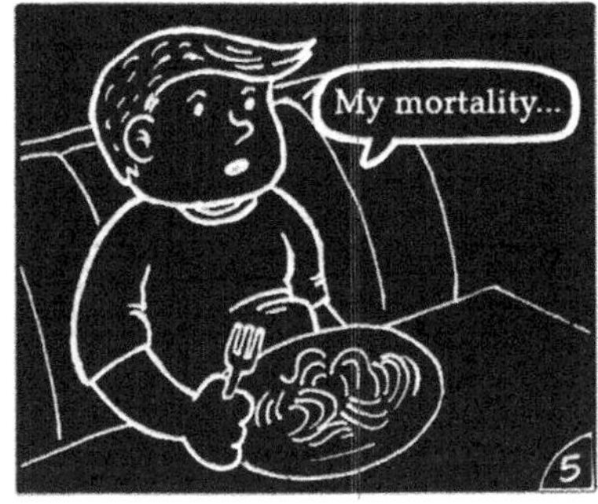

Hamburger Circus

"Can I go to camp?"
"Sure... when dogs learn how to talk."
"Thank you, foster mom."

The Family Jewels

"I want a new dog."
"All your dogs turn up missing.
Now eat your dinner."

Hamburger Circus

The Family Jewels

"What is it?"

A tranquil sunset?
A cosmic phenomenon?
A smurf massacre.

Catabolysis

A rare speciman:
The Venus Cannibal-Trap
and nearly extinct.

"What is it?"

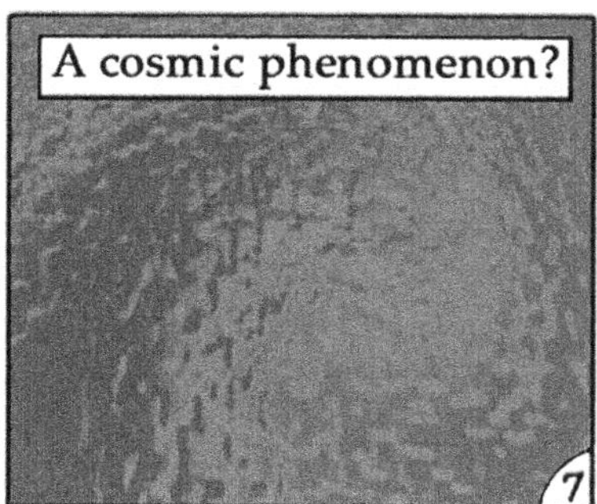

Catabolysis

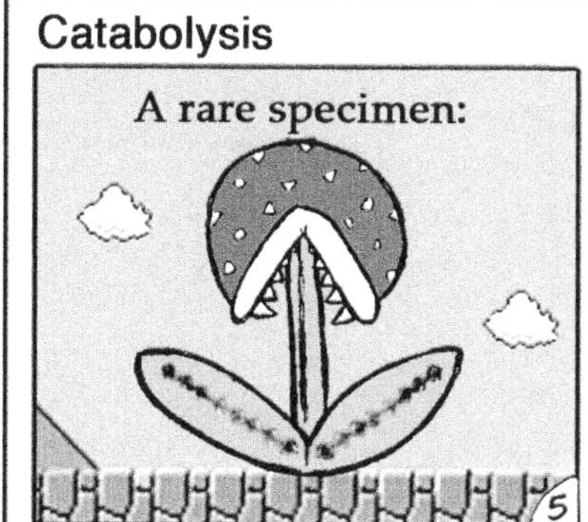

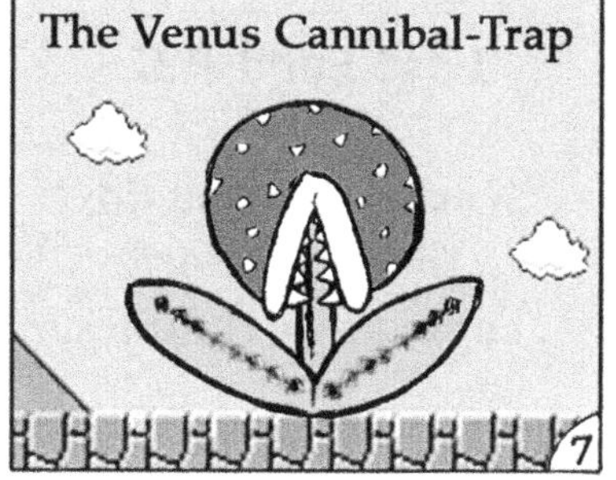

Chess Pieces Saying Movie Quotes

"I love you." "Ditto."
"Hasta la vista, baby."
"Get in my belly!"

Fast Food P.C.

Kosher McDonalds
100% No Pork
Toys for the kiddies.

Chess Pieces Saying Movie Quotes

Fast Food P.C.

Kid Doodles

Here's a mustar-stache.
And of course he needs a bee-rd.
Ooh, I know... sideburns.

5.
NON-SEQUITARS

"How's your glaucoma, Grandpa Joe?"

"Today's my birthday.
And nobody remembered."
"Surprise!" "It's Thumbers!"

Overreacting

"I thought 'everything'
was two words. But it's just one!"
Then his head blew up.

“How’s your glaucoma, Grandpa Joe.”

Overreacting

Clipart Rodeo

"Sales are through the roof."
"First, America. Then we
take over the world!"

The Bad Neighborhood Kid

Hey, Mr. Turtle.
I want you to meet my friend.
Corporal Hammer!

Clipart Rodeo

The Bad Neighborhood Kid

Drugs vs. Vegetables

"I'll get them to play:
'Seven Minutes in Heaven'."
"Leave those teens alone!"

Emoticons for the Blind

Away from keyboard.
F*cked up beyond all reason.
Laughing my ass off.

Drugs vs. Vegetables

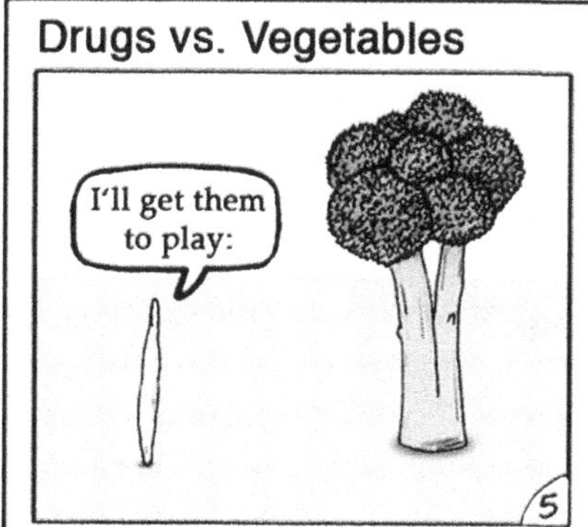

Emoticons for the Blind

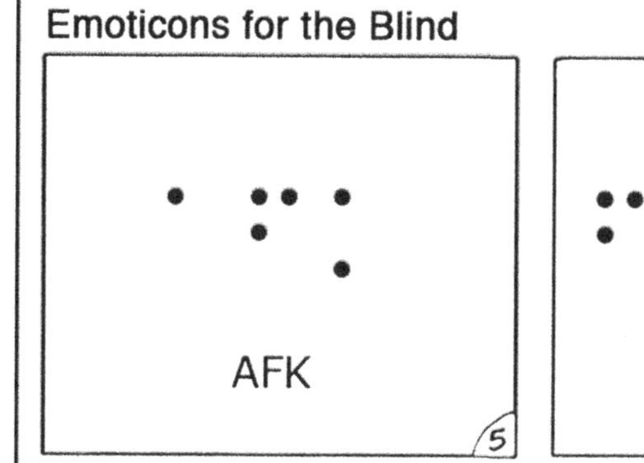

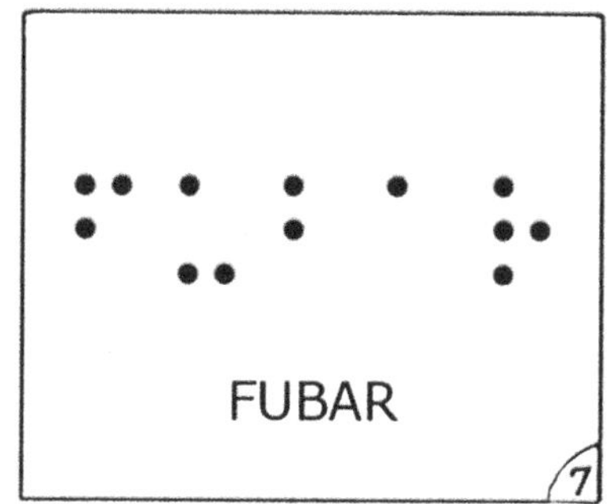

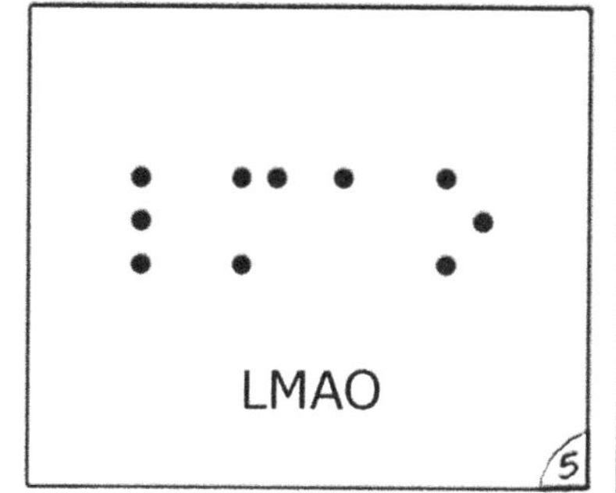

Bowling Ball Nightmares

"Help!!! I'm infested!"
"The kids laugh 'cause I'm half-pin."
7-90 Split.

Mutually Assured Party

Nuclear missiles...
...are a threat to mankind. But...
...the atom digs it!

Bowling Ball Nightmares

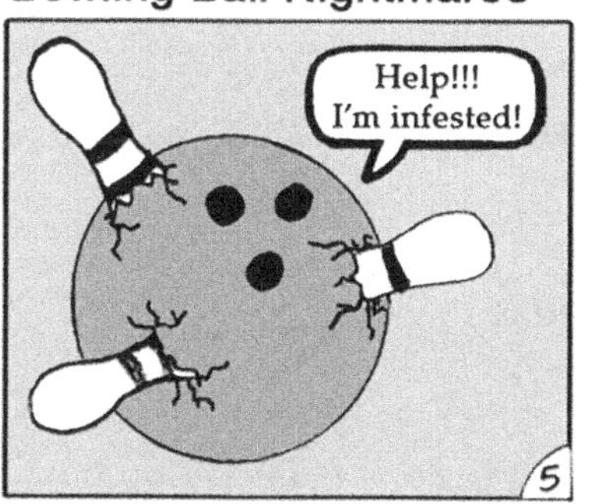

Mutually Assured Party

Looking for a Few Good Men

Uncle Sam wants you.
Yes. That's right... You! I want you...
...to smell my finger.

"Out here we is stoned... Immaculate."

There once was a rock
that thought it was an oak tree.
I'm flippin' out, yo!

Looking for a Few Good Men

"Out here we is stoned... Immaculate."

There once was a rock...

The Continuing Saga of Blake and Kid

Two unlikely friends.
Blake is a carbon atom!
Kid is a donkey!

Secret Agent Stuff

This man is a spy.
He rides a spy bicycle.
You guessed it... spy boots.

The Continuing Saga of Blake and Kid

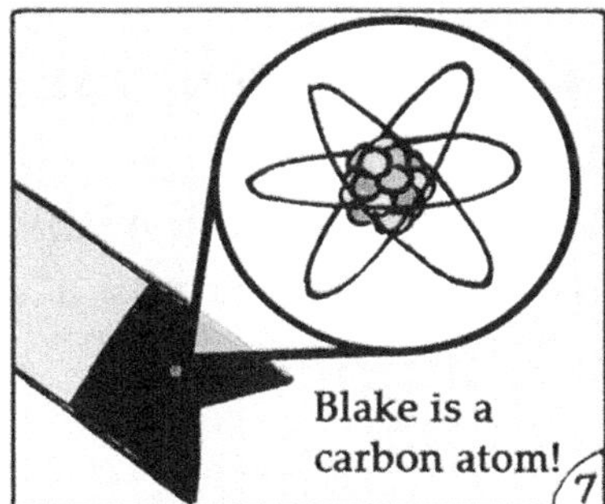

"I got an F on my Earth Sciences report."

"When clouds think of things
their thoughts make more clouds. Those clouds..."
See me.

Grammar Murder

'Z' didn't like 'A'.
So... 'Z' pushed 'A' off a cliff.
Znd thzt's whzt hzppened.

Grammar Murder

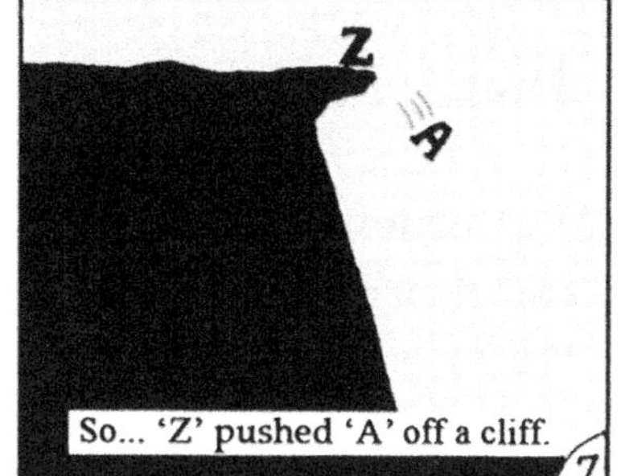

Covered in Leeches

I could remove them.
But I kind of like how they
make me feel wanted.

Theory of Relativity

"We're short one player."
"Aw, crap. Here comes that new kid
with the birth defect."

Covered in Leeches

Theory of Relativity

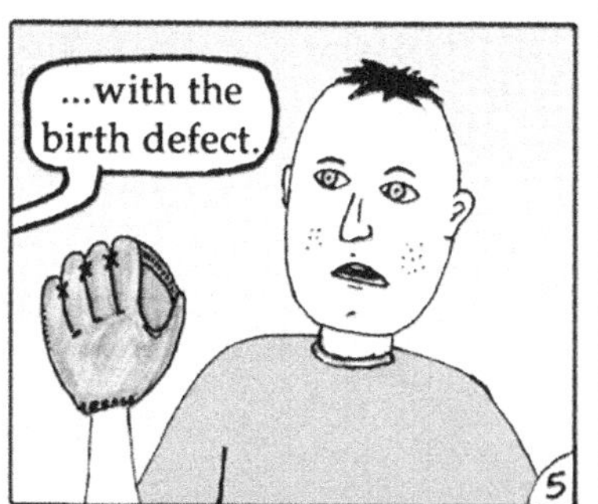

Recipe for "Smores Over Time"

Noon: eat chocolate.
6pm: a graham cracker.
Bedtime: marshmallows.

Phoning it In

Hmmm... What should I draw?
Arrrrrrrrgh!!! Damn this "creative drought"!
Pig in a rocket.

Recipe for "Smores Over Time"

Phoning it In

Schizophrenia

"Been here a long time
and..." Hi, Fred." "I'm hearing things."
"Who said that? Who's there?"

Puberty: Your Changing Body

Get milk. "I'm falling."
Add bacteria. Ferment.
"Where... nay, what am I?"

Schizophrenia

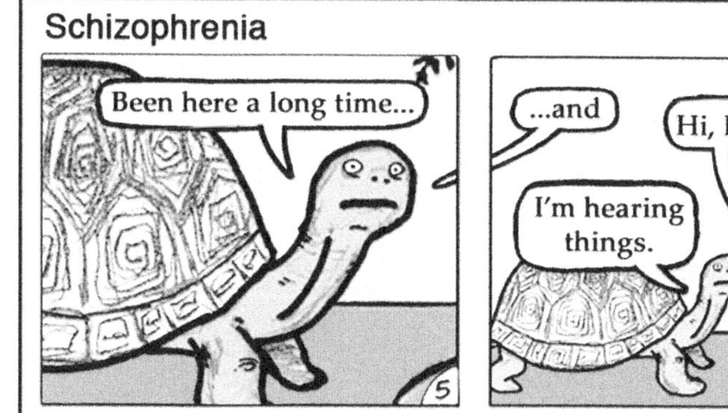

Puberty: Your Changing Body

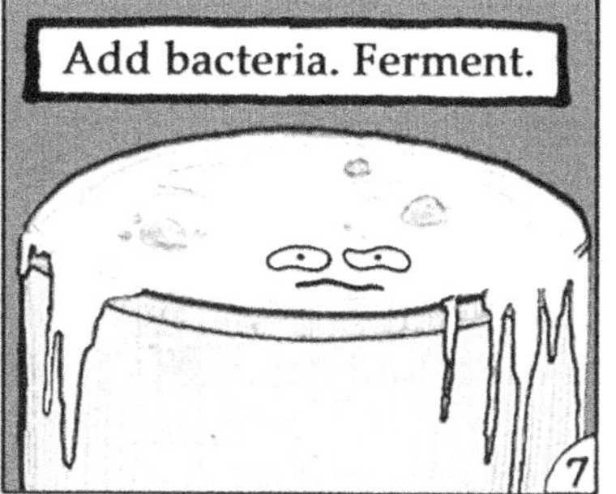

A Christmas Miracle

"Who put coal in here?
Where's the rest of my presents?!"
"This can keep me warm."

"Where do they learn these things?"

"So how was the zoo?"
"Fine." "Just fine? What did you learn?"
"We watched monkeys pork."

A Christmas Miracle
Who put coal in here?
5
Where's the rest of my presents?!
7
This can keep me warm.
5

"Where do they learn these things?"
So how was the zoo?
5
Fine.
Just fine?
What did you learn?
7
We watched monkeys pork.
5

"If I did it... *If* I stole the candy, which I didn't."

I would have grabbed it
and put it in my pocket.
But I'm innocent.

Kid Answers to Adult Problems

For global warming
we should put a huge ice cube
on the Earth's forehead.

"If I did it... *If* I stole the candy, which I didn't."

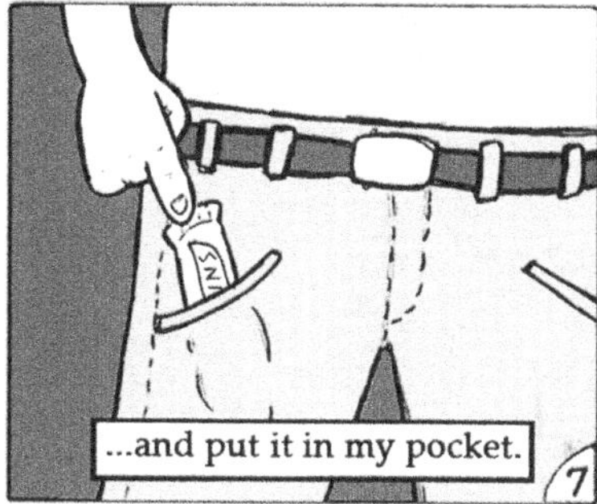

Kid Answers to Adult Problems

6.
MELANCHOLY

Pessimistic Child

Each year, asthma kills
5,000 children. Am I
five thousand and one?

A Definition of Love

Cockroach of the sea.
One day you'll grow up to be...
Food that is pricey!

Pessimistic Child

A Definition of Love

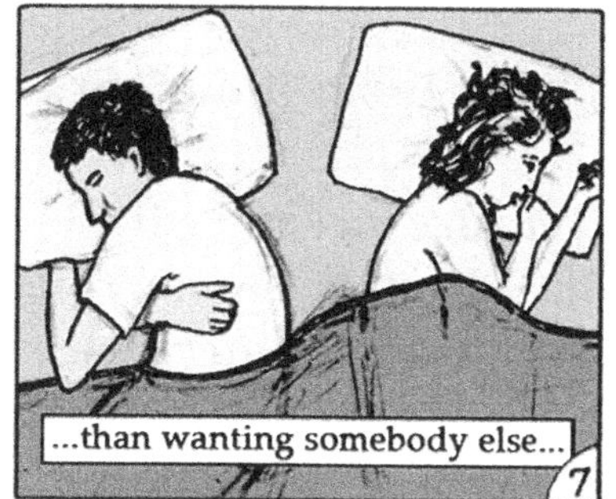

"He died doing what he loved."

My dearest Simone
you complete me... forever.
Will you marry me?

Carpe Diem Dinosaurs

"I sure love my wife."
"But I'll tell her tomorrow."
Meanwhile... outer space

"He died doing what he loved."

My dearest Simone
you complete me... forever...
Will you marry me

Show and Tell

Here's my sticker book.
I don't get to collect much
since I'm very poor.

Grape Romance

"I love you so much."
"My love for you is boundless."
"To be young again."

Show and Tell

Grape Romance

All Aboard

"Goodbye Anthony."
"It's probably for the best."
Little do they know...

Stick Man

Just keep barking, Rex.
Someone is bound to find you.
Goodbye Cruel World

All Aboard

Stick Man

"That's the day we lost dad."

"That was inhumane.
For all we know today is
Cockroach Thanksgiving."

Family Ties

Here's my family.
Kevin, mom, me and Snuggles.
Here is my daddy.

"That's the day we lost dad."

Family Ties

Time is Time is Time

When will it be noon?
When will it be 5 o'clock?
Will it ever end?

Shattered Car Windshield

Got glass in my eyes.
So now all I can do is
listen to music.

Time is Time is Time

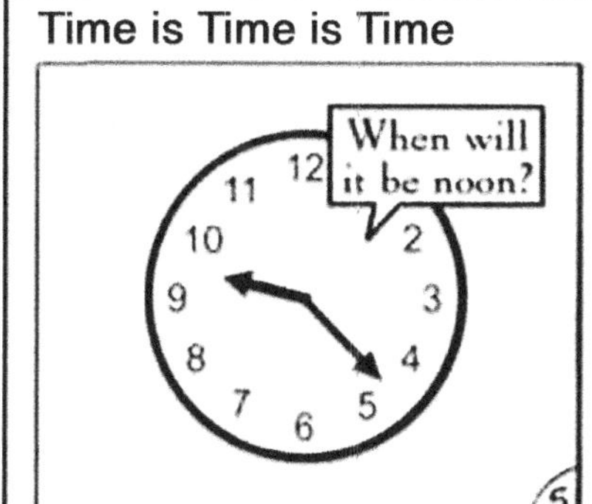

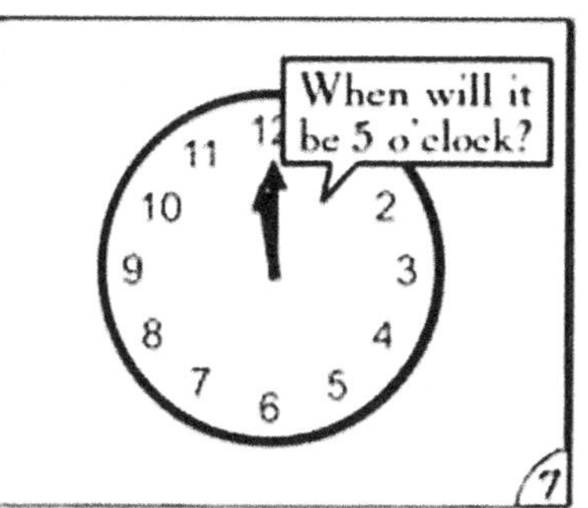

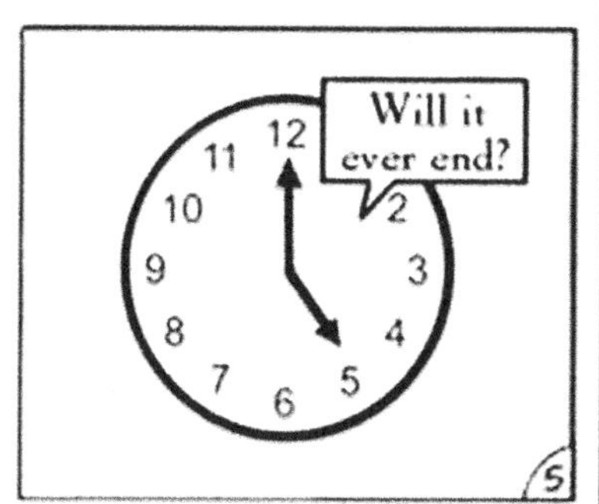

Shattered Car Windshield

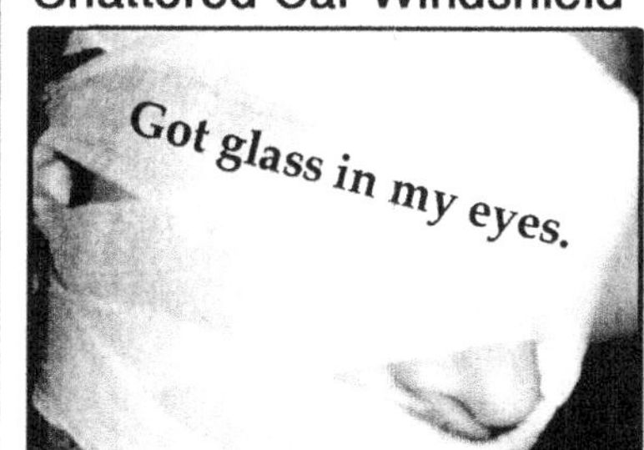

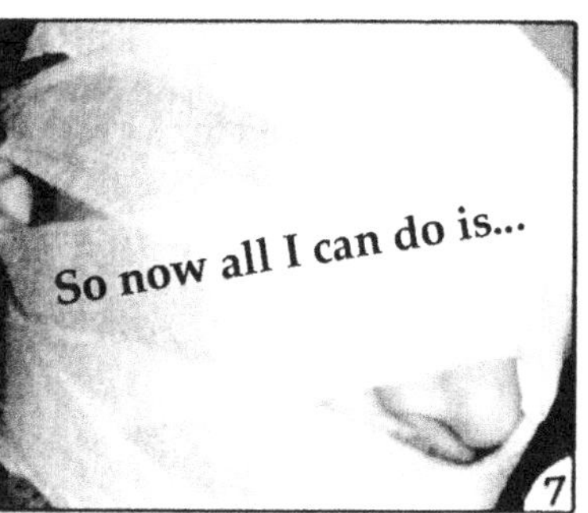

MARSHMALLOW HEADS
7.

Another Advantage of Living in Fun Town

"What is for dinner?"
"Omelets." "Breakfast for dinner?!"
"Welcome to Fun Town."

"That works on so many levels."

"Knock, knock." "Who's there?" "Ted."
"Ted who?" "Help, I got no arms!"
"You should do stand-up."

Another Advantage of Living in Fun Town
What is for dinner?
5
Omelets.
Breakfast for dinner?!
7
Welcome to Fun Town.
5

"That works on so many levels."
Knock, knock.
Who's There?
Ted.
5
Ted who?
Help, I got no arms!
7
You should do stand-up.
5

Escape from the Belly of a Whale

"We could build a fire."
"Let's give him dysentery."
"Face it. We're stuck here."

Moby Dorks

"We're still alive." "Check."
"We're trapped but things could be worse."
"A shark in a whale!!"

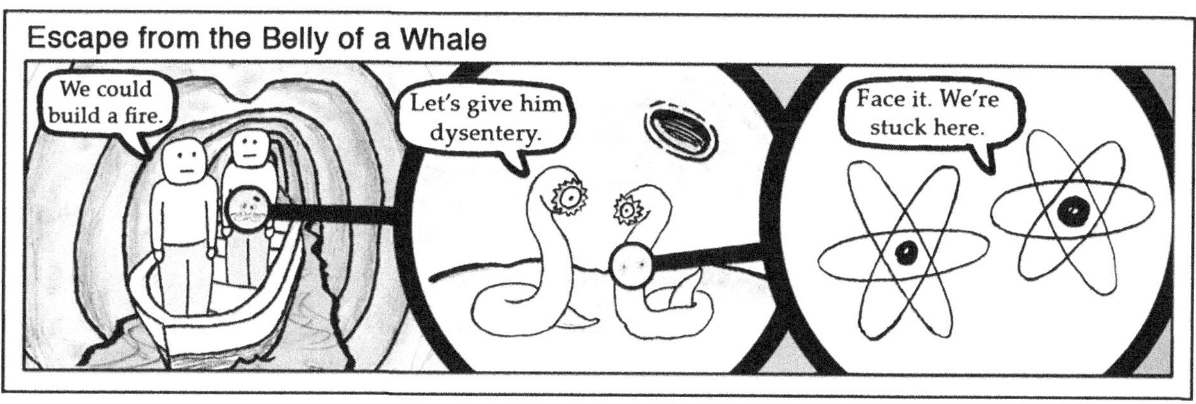
Escape from the Belly of a Whale
We could build a fire.
Let's give him dysentery.
Face it. We're stuck here.

Moby Dorks
We're still alive.
Check.
5
We're trapped but things could be worse.
7
A shark in a whale!!
5

Nonsense

"Who's on first." "Uh-huh."
"What's on second." "Where's the bus?"
"I don't know." "Haha!"

They Walk Among Us

"You're one of them." "Who?"
"The Pod-People!" "No, I'm not.
Are you?" "Curses! Foiled!!"

Nonsense

They Walk Among Us

A Bad Joke

"I don't know. What is
red and causes a sharp pain?"
"A bloody ax." "Oh."

Get Well Soon

"I got you flowers."
"Where are they?" "Gone. I got mugged."
"You owe me flowers."

A Bad Joke

I don't know. What is...

5

...red and causes a sharp pain?

7

A bloody ax.

Oh.

5

Meteor Shower

"There's another one!"
"Why do I keep missing them?
Oh, right. 'Cuz I'm blind."

"It snowed last night!"

"There's no show outside."
"It's imagination snow
and you made it melt!"

Meteor Shower
There's another one!
5
Why do I keep missing them?
7
Oh, right. 'Cuz I'm blind!
5

"It snowed last night!"
There's no snow outside.
5
It's imagination snow...
7
And you made it melt!
5

8.
ANTHROPOMORPHISM

Stan Cocktail

"Try the shrimp," they say.
I have a name. You hear me?
You're eating Stan... Stan!

Male Spiders can be Such Pigs

"Hey there good looking.
Those legs go all the way up?"
"Neat. It still moves." "Aaargh!"

Stan Cocktail

"Try the shrimp," they say.

5

Male Spiders can be Such Pigs

Take These Broken Wings

“Hey, Hank.” “Word up, bro.”
“Can I help you carry that?”
What birds dream about.

Peace Frog

Listen up, hippies.
Quit licking me to get high.
Lick yourselves! I do.

Take These Broken Wings

Peace Frog

Addicted to People

"Where have you been?" "Work."
"Lies! I smell blood on your breath --
out eating surfers!"

"Hey yo, Tooth Fairy!"

Lost one of my teeth.
Did the Tooth Fairy come? No.
I want my quarter.

Addicted to People

"Hey yo, Tooth Fairy!"

*#%@$

"Ribbet! We're so dead."
"Oh, oink! This is all your fault."
"Who the moo broke that!?"

Nothing's Gonna Stop Us Now

"Fine. You're a decoy...
But dammit I still love you!"
"That made me real."

*#%@$

Nothing's Gonna Stop Us Now

Slug Fest

"Baby. Like that?" "More."
"Right there?" "That's the spot. Do it."
"I love you." "Oh, crap."

Butterfly Kisses

"People-kiss me, Frank."
"It's forbidden. We'll get caught.
We mustn't." "Mustn't."

Slug Fest
Like that?
Baby.
More.
5
Right there?
That's the spot.
Do it.
7
I love you.
Oh, crap.
5

Butterfly Kisses
People-kiss me, Frank.
5
It's forbidden. We'll get caught.
7
We mustn't.
Mustn't.
5

Nake & Brabbit

"You should move in." "Whoa...
commitment." "It'll be fun."
"Sweet. We have cable."

Wild Kingdom

The lewd behavior
North American tree frog
says: "Rubbit, rubbit."

Nake & Brabbit

Wild Kingdom

"Why does the female praying mantis eat the male after they mate?"

She bites off the head
so dad can see the children
and tell them stories!

Fickle Moo Moo

I was like, emo.
Then, you know, punk exploded.
But now I'm metal.

"Why does the female praying mantis eat the male after they mate?"

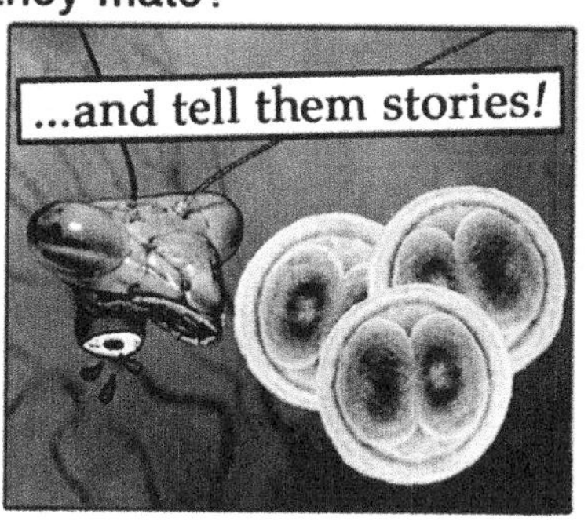

Fickle Moo Moo

A Common Myth About Spiders

We don't eat our young.
They just jump into our mouths.
Stop it! Babies! No!

Dirty, Old Rabbit

One time years ago
I rode this broad for six hours.
Hey, where you going?

A Common Myth About Spiders

Dirty, Old Rabbit

"Nothing more to see here."

**"Do I smell dinner?"
"It's coming from over there."
"Damn." "We just missied it."**

"Buster, no!"

**The rare goldfish-cat:
If you overfeed them, they
eat until they die.**

"Nothing more to see here."

Do I smell dinner?
5

It's coming from over there.
7

Damn.
We just missed it.
CRIME SCENE
DO NOT CROSS
5

"Buster, no!"

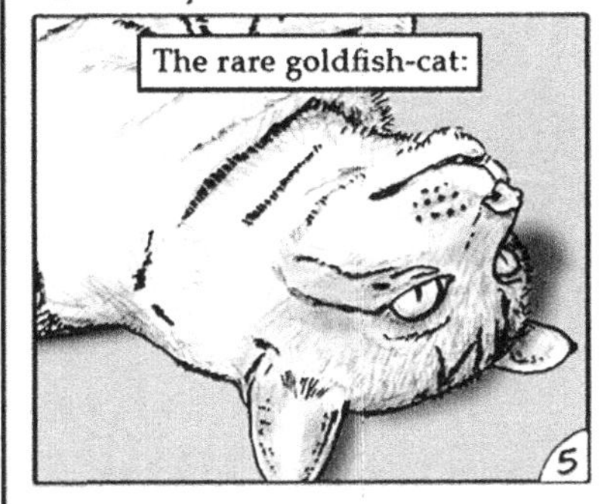
The rare goldfish-cat:
5

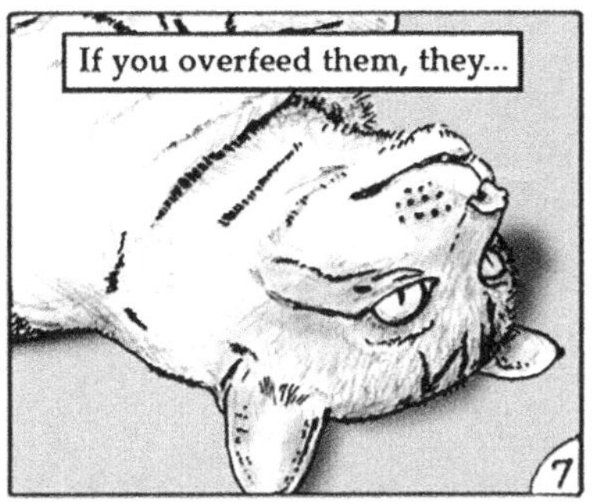
If you overfeed them, they...
7

...eat until they die.
5

"I wish I may, I wish I might..."

"...a real goldfish."
"Don't stop dreaming, kid. Don't stop..."
KA-ZAAM "I can't breathe."

Coyboy

"Ride you all night long?
Gee... I don't know. It sounds fun."
"Maybe you'll like it."

"I wish I may, I wish I might..."

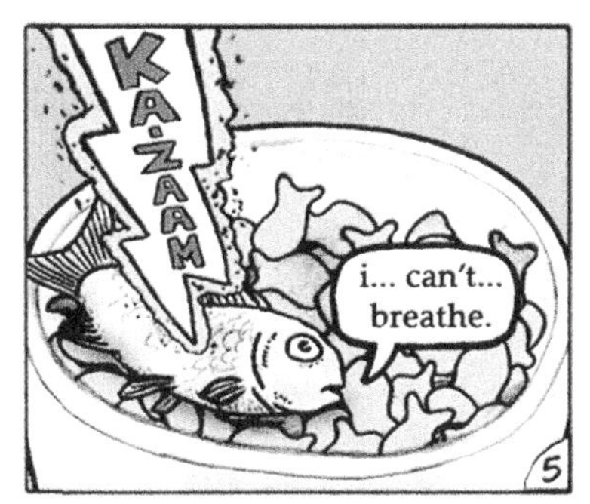

Coyboy

"And now a word from our sponsor."

I smoke Marbolos.
All-natural cigarettes.
Now that's "Full Flavor".

The Misadventures of Nake and Brabbit

"Let's not." "C'mon, man
yummy people food!" LATER...
"You're an herbivore?"

"And now a word from our sponsor."

The Misadventures of Nake and Brabbit

The Only Known Sound That Does Not Echo

That was the last straw!
I won't take it anymore!
Do you hear me?! Huh?!?

Cell Division

"Billy, where are you?
Has anyone seen my son?"
"Here I am mommy."

The Only Known Sound That Does Not Echo

That was the last straw!

5

I won't take it anymore!

7

DO YOU HEAR ME?! HUH?!?

5

Cell Division

9.
JUXTAPOSITION

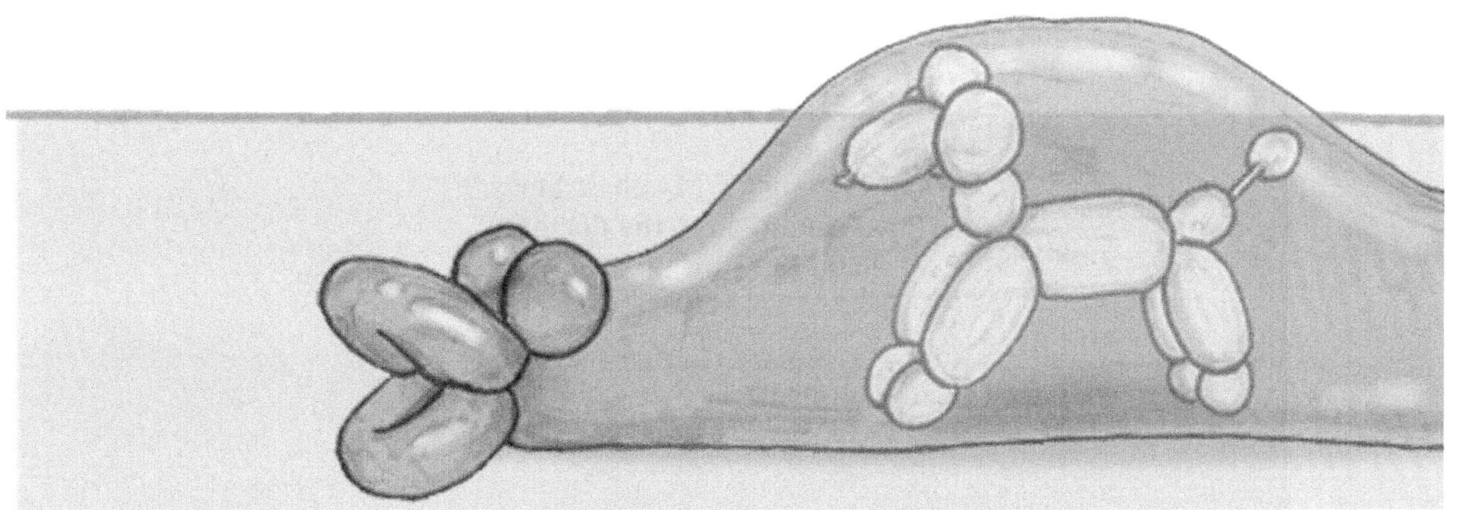

Friday Nights at St. Joseph's

**"I – 18, B – 5...
O – 74..." "Bingo!"
"That's a good bingo."**

Heart Attack Warning Signs

**"What's wrong?" "My chest hurts."
"You should go to the doctor
could be your giblets."**

Friday Nights at St. Joseph's

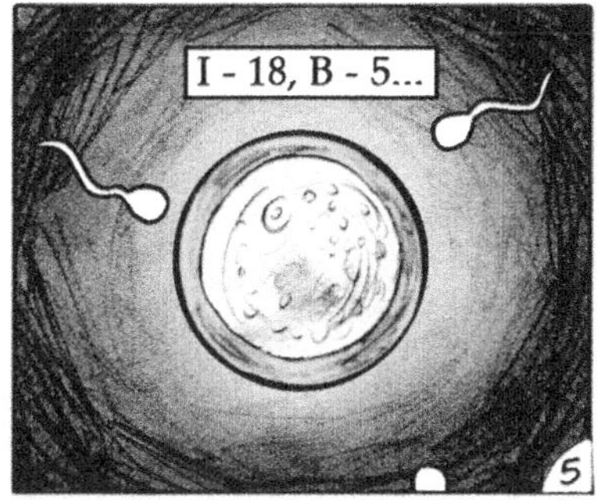

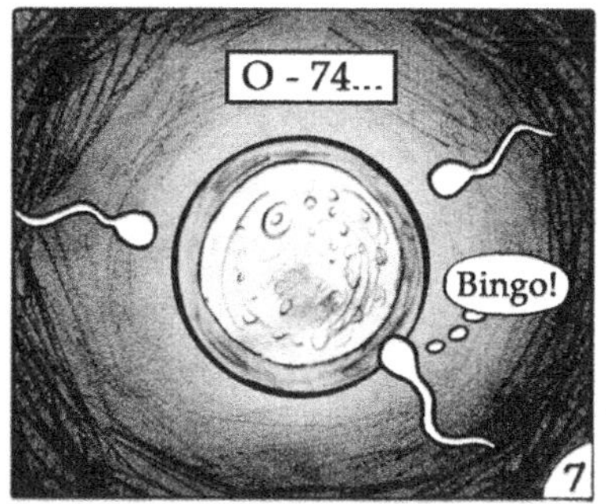

Heart Attack Warning Signs

Touchy-Feely Science

Light Experiment.
Is it waves or particles?
Microscopic Fish!

Reincarnation

"The Worm Monarchy
has gone too far!" "Yes, but who...
who will lead us?" "Who?"

Touchy-Feely Science

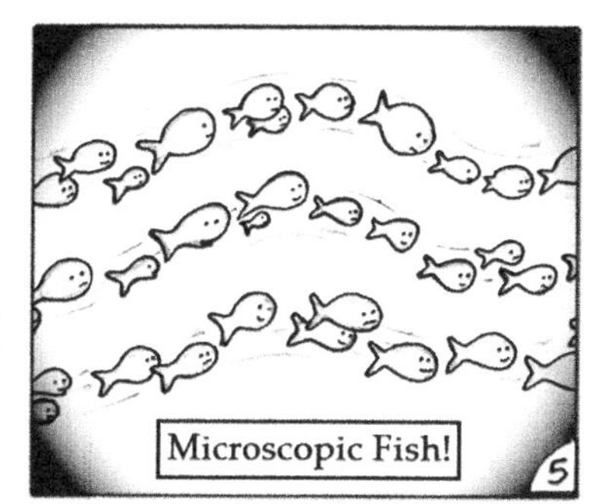

Reincarnation

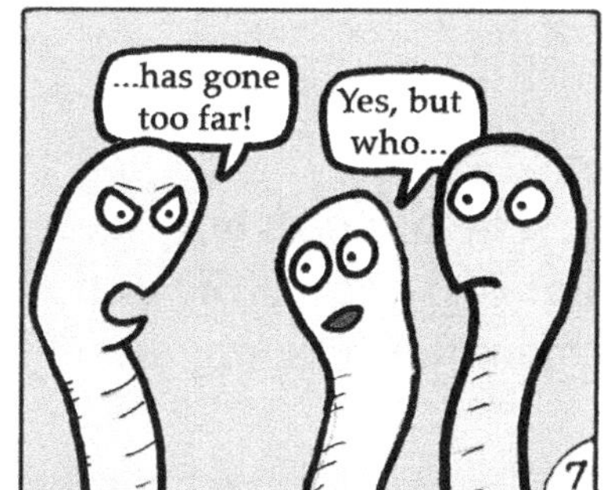

“We’re saved!”

Shape Squad, mobilize!
Form of... The Battle Wagon!
Take that, Polygon!

Sudoku Circus

The hot puzzle craze
that is sweeping the nation.
“You don’t belong here.”

"We're saved!"

Sudoku Circus

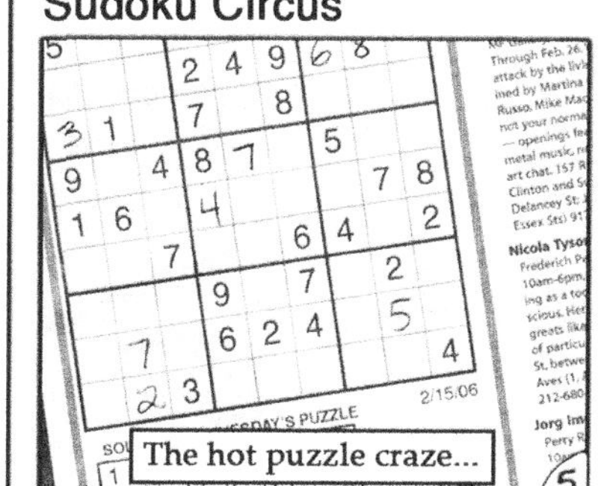

"I've never seen a case like it."

"Now, Mr. Jenkins...
What seems to be the problem?"
"I'm vomiting words!"

Thumbs Up to Ya!

Keep it up, Police!
Looking good there, Firefighters!
Nice work, Lumberjacks!

"I've never seen a case like it."

Thumbs Up to Ya!

"To see, or not to sell the farm..."

"There's oil on this land...
You could make a fortune, friend"
"Parlez vous anglais?"*

Marine Biology

Microscopic sperm.
Here is a giant sperm whale.
Little sperm whale sperms.

*You speak English?

"To sell, or not to sell the farm..."

Marine Biology

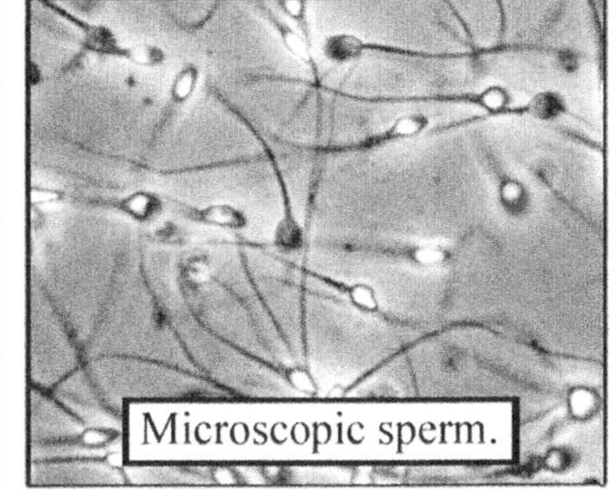

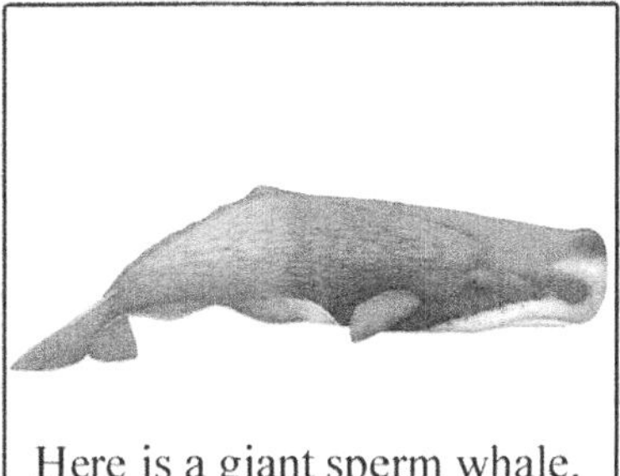

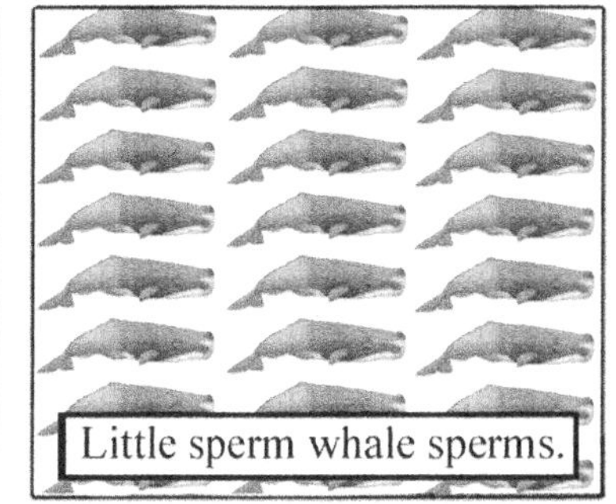

Sock Puppet Coroner

I have to warn you...
This ain't a pretty sight, sir.
You can see his brains!

Ka-BOOM!

What's wrong there, Marty?
Come out. We'll talk about it.
Hey. You're not Marty!

Sock Puppet Coroner

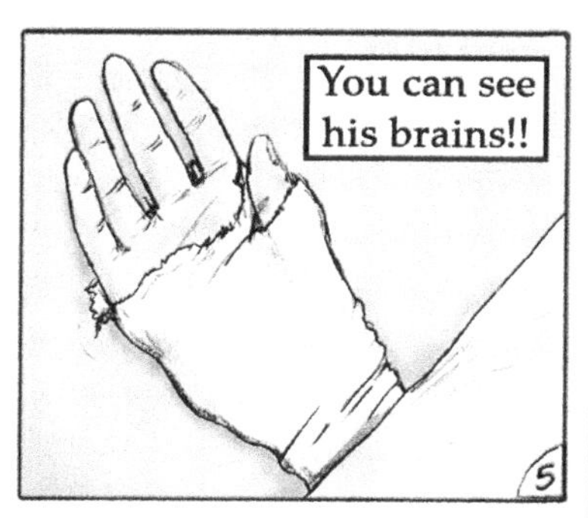

Ka-*BOOM!*

Balloon Animals

The python shadows
an unsuspecting poodle,
and swallows her whole.

Prune Hands

"They'll soak overnight."
"I want those dishes washed now!"
"But we like to soak."

Balloon Animals

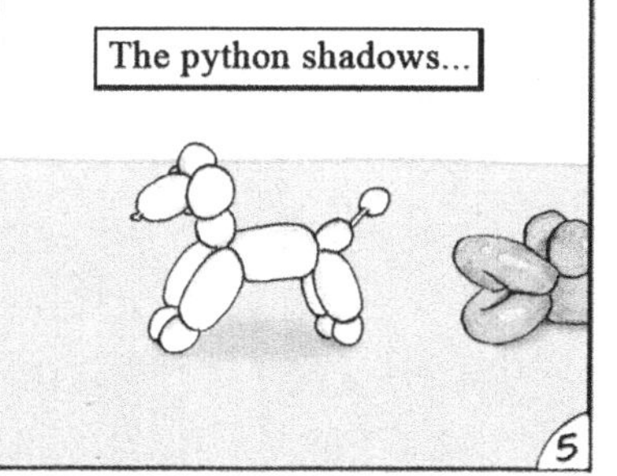

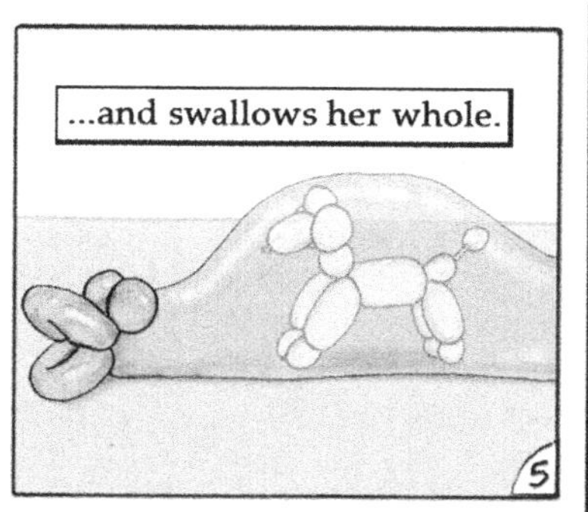

Prune Hands

Bunny Alligator

"Oh, man... I'm starving.
This was a bad idea."
"Can I hug you?" "Score."

Hang Ten! High Five!

"So I said to him,
'No you're the jerk.' Then he said..."
"Man, this guy's a tool."

Bunny Alligator

Hang Ten! High Five!

The Great Escape

"Look... an oasis!"
"C'mon boys, we're saved." "Yee-haw!"
"Help us! The burning!"

The Great Escape, cont.

"There. In the sky!" "God?"
"Tell me, God... why are we here?
Arghhh... Have mercy, Lord."

The Great Escape
Look... an oasis!
5
C'mon boys, we're saved.
Yee-haw!
OOKIES
7
Help us!
The burning!
5

The Great Escape, cont.
There. In the sky!
God?
5
Tell me, God... why are we here?
7
Arghhh... Have mercy, Lord.
5

The Great Escape, part 3

"Go on... save yourselves!"
"Stop it. Stop! You're killing him!
Hang in there. Ted? Ted!!"

10.
YEAR ONE

Untitled

"What are you doing?"
FACT: Fish have poor memories.
"What are you doing?"

Cough Syrup

This stuff tastes better
the second or third time down.
A NyQuil-holic

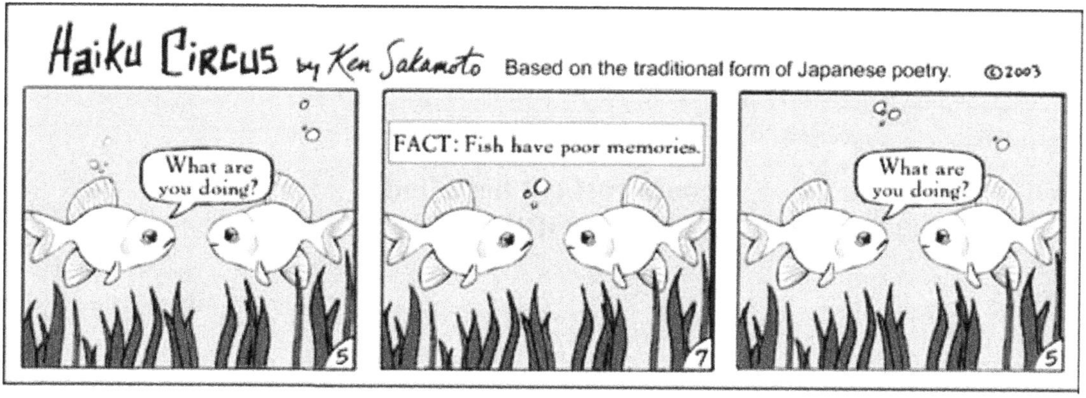
Haiku Circus by Ken Sakamoto
Based on the traditional form of Japanese poetry.
©2003
What are you doing?
5
FACT: Fish have poor memories.
7
What are you doing?
5

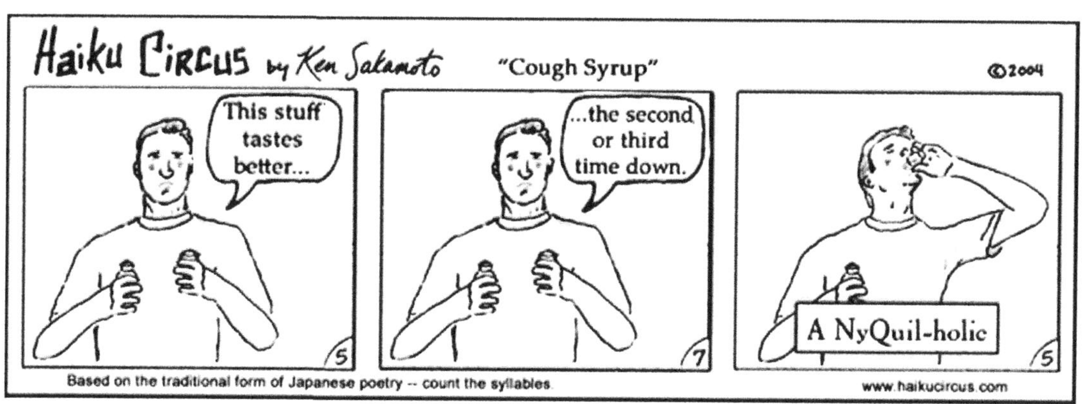
Haiku Circus by Ken Sakamoto
"Cough Syrup"
©2004
This stuff tastes better...
5
...the second or third time down.
7
A NyQuil-holic
5
Based on the traditional form of Japanese poetry -- count the syllables.
www.haikucircus.com

“My niece is so cute.
I could just eat her all up.”
GOBBLE GOBBLE “Yum!”

What is your problem?
Haven’t you seen a baboon
smoke a pipe before?

Haiku Circus by Ken Sakamoto Based on the traditional form of Japanese poetry. ©2003
My niece is so cute.
5
I could just eat her all up.
7
GOBBLE
GOBBLE
YUM!
5

Haiku Circus by Ken Sakamoto Based on the traditional form of Japanese poetry. ©2003
What is your problem?
5
Haven't you seen a baboon...
7
...smoke a pipe before?
5
www.haikucircus.com

Take one coconut.
Crack open with a hammer.
Then make into a bra.

"You smell." "You smell more!"
"You are the worst smell on Earth."
"You both reek. Say, "Ahh."

Haiku Circus by Ken Sakamoto Based on the traditional form of Japanese poetry. ©2003
Take one coconut.
5
Crack open with a hammer.
7
Then make into bra.
5

Haiku Circus by Ken Sakamoto Count the syllables, thank you. ©2003
You smell.
You smell more!
5
You are the worst smell on Earth.
7
You both reek. Say, "Ahh."
5

click click click ding click
"I hate being a robot."
click click click click click

"We could play boardgames.
We could go on a picnic."
"I'd rather stand here."

Haiku Circus by Ken Sakamoto
Based on the traditional form of Japanese poetry.
©2003
click click click
ding click
5
I hate being a robot.
7
click click click
click
click...
5

Haiku Circus by Ken Sakamoto
Count the syllables, thank you.
©2003
We could play boardgames.
5
We could go on a picnic.
7
I'd rather stand here.
5

It may be boring
to watch paint dry, 'tis much worse
to be drying paint.

Must eat brains. Brains. Brains.
Brains. Brains. Brains. Wait. I forgot.
Oh yeah, brains. Brains. Brains...

Haiku Circus by Ken Sakamoto
Based on the traditional form of Japanese poetry.
©2003
It may be boring
5
to watch paint dry. 'tis much worse. . .
7
to be drying paint.
5
PAINT

Haiku Circus by Ken Sakamoto
Based on the traditional form of Japanese poetry.
©2003
Must eat brains. Brains. Brains.
5
Brains. Brains. Brains. Wait. I forgot.
7
Oh yeah. brains. Brains. Brains..
5

Will you be my friend?
We can sing, dance, do magic.
Deceived you, I have.

"Why are we here, star?"
"Some of us shine, others fall."
"You should write that down."

Haiku Circus by Ken Sakamoto
Based on the traditional form of Japanese poetry.
©2003
Will you be my friend?
5
We can sing, dance, do magic.
7
Deceived you, I have.
5
www.haikucircus.com

Haiku Circus by Ken Sakamoto
Count the syllables, thank you.
©2003
Why are we here, star?
5
Some of us shine, others fall.
7
You should write that down.
5

THE END?
HAIKU
CIRCUS
2003 - 2009

Why a book now.

Summer 2011 - a friend called me up to say he stumbled upon the Haiku Circus collection on Amazon and he wanted to give his congrats. I knew nothing about it. So I searched Amazon and found a book published out of South Africa available for $50. If they can put out a book, why can't the original author? Plus I always told myself that perhaps Haiku Circus was just on a temporary hiatus, that I'd start it up again when the time was right. Perhaps this Vol 1. collection will jumpstart a reboot.

P.S. I initially hesitated in reporting the copyright infringement, choosing to leave it up as motivation to get the "real" layout finalized. It has since mysteriously been removed.

Why I used a pseudonym.

I never liked comic strips. With the exception of *Calvin and Hobbes, The Far Side, Red Meat, Derf*, and some others I'm forgetting - I generally considered the art form trite and snarky. So when I first came up with the idea of drawing pictures to haikus I thought by using a fake name I absolved myself (or at least distanced myself) from any comic strip-hating hypocrisy.

Second, I thought a Japanese name would somehow legitimize these versions of Americanized pseudo haikus. Did you know there are some people out there who get angry over the 5-7-5 syllable structure?

Lastly, it was modesty... or self-doubt over my ability to draw consistently well. It turned out to be a double-edged sword... Being Ken Sakamoto gave me the freedom to try things new, step out of my comfort zone but allowed me to get lazy and phone some in. It was also fun to have a secret project, a small success to quietly celebrate. It used to be important to me to protect that secret, but not anymore. I've changed my mind... such is life.

About the author.

While writing and drawing Haiku Circus between 2003 – 2009, Shawn Wickens also spent some of his free time road tripping across the country interviewing people about their first time for his first book, *How to Lose Your Virginity (...and how not to).* He is from Cleveland, lives in New York and performs weekly at the Magnet Theater with the improv group Junior Varsity.

SPECIAL THANKS TO...

Johnny Wu and MDI for providing my very first Haiku Circus office space.
Second City Cleveland (R.I.P.) for getting me to write more. Doug Fill for being my first model (NyQuil-holic). Peter Guren for early comic strip advice. Zach and the Starnik sisters (you know your names) plus Dave Smialek and Sean Robinson (and Doug again) ...you're all muses. Melissa Bird for always reminding me when I "accidentally" spit gum in your hair. Jason Calicchia for introducing me to NYC, which still continues to pay off. My early UCB teachers (George Badecker, Brian Huskey, Julie Brister and Jason Mantzoukas) for dragging me from behind the page and on the stage. The Whites of Their Eyes (Starr Kendall, David Levin, Yang Miller and Chris O'Neil) for giving me a change to Primal Scream. Donna Jewell for sharing her enthusiasm. The Magnet Theater and Armando Diaz, Ed Herbstman, Alex Marino, Peter McNerney for creating a great venue and community. The 100+ website visitors who bought t-shirts. All the newspapers. Rick Koston – best co-host ever. The PIT, Ali Farahnakian for having an open stage where anyone can perform, all the Improdome regulars and original hosts – Diana DePasquale and Mark Grenier. All of my bros and hos on Junior Varsity (Lucia Aniello, Jarret Berenstein, Jane Borden, Kevin Cragg, Megan Gray, Lex Morales, Jamie Rivera, Sean Taylor) for the best road trips a growing boy could have. Megan Gray (who deserves an extra shout out) whose name, as it turns out, was left off a previous thank you list – keep on keeping it real, lobster harmonica. My main wildcats Joe Buccier and Dan Spahr. Jaqueline Fouasnon for leading when we dance.

Made in the USA
Middletown, DE
16 April 2022